EARTH'S CHANGING LANDSCAPE

Rivers in Action

Mary Green

A+

First published in 2003 by Franklin Watts
Franklin Watts, 96 Leonard Street, London EC2A 4XD

Franklin Watts Australia
45–51 Huntley Street, Alexandria, NSW 2015
This edition published under license from Franklin Watts.
 All rights reserved.

Copyright © 2003 Franklin Watts

Series Editor: Sarah Peutrill; Series Designer: Simon Borrough; Art Director: Jonathan Hair; Picture Researcher: Juliet Duff; Illustrations: Ian Thompson; Series Consultant: Steve Watts, FRGS, Principal Lecturer in Geography Education at the University of Sunderland

Published in the United States by Smart Apple Media
1980 Lookout Drive, North Mankato, Minnesota 56003

U.S. publication copyright © 2005 Smart Apple Media
International copyright reserved in all countries. No part of
this book may be reproduced in any form without written permission from the publisher.

Library of Congress Cataloging-in-Publication Data

Green, Mary, 1947–
Rivers in action / by Mary Green.
p. cm. — (Earth's changing landscape)
Summary: Explores the different forces that act to change rivers' courses, including the effect of humans in the process and what can be done to lessen our impact.
ISBN 1-58340-477-5
1. Rivers—Juvenile literature. 2. Stream ecology—Juvenile literature. 3. Human geography—Juvenile literature. [1. Rivers. 2. Stream ecology. 3. Ecology. 4. Nature—Effect of human beings on.] I. Title. II. Series.

GB1203.8.G74 2004
551.48'3—dc22   2003066197

9 8 7 6 5 4 3 2 1

Picture Credits:
Alamy Images: 33 Robert Harding Picture Library; 40 Leslie Garland Picture Library. Corbis: 24 Robert Holmes; 32 Craig Aurness. James Davis Travel Photography: 22, 25. Digital Vision: endpapers and 10, 18, 31, 34, 38, 39 (both). Ecoscene: 11 Joel Creed; 14 David Wootton Photography; 20 Colin Convoy; 27 (bottom) Christine Osborne; 28–29 Alexandra Jones; 30 Chinch Gryniewicz; 42 Anthony Cooper. Eye Ubiquitous: 8 Judyth Platt; 16, 37 (bottom) Julia Waterlow; 17, 23 J. B. Pickering; 19 Stephen Rafferty, 21 L. Fordyce (top), 26 Chris Fairclough. Chris Fairclough Photography: 13. Holt Studios International: 43 Mike Lane. Photodisc: 6, 21 (bottom). Still Pictures: 12 Martin Hawes; 15, 36, 41 Mark Edwards; 18-19 Dylan Garcia, 27 (top) Hjalte Tin; 29 Toby Adamson; 35 Paul Glendell, 37 (top) Jorgen Schytte.
Front Cover: Ecoscene/Joel Creed.

CONTENTS

RIVERS AND THE WATER CYCLE

Two-thirds of Earth is covered with water. It is essential to all living things on the planet, but water also has a dramatic effect on Earth's landscape. Rivers, in particular, have shaped many of the most spectacular landscape features of the world, provided fertile land for farming, and even determined where people live.

In the beginning Water was formed from gases millions of years ago. Most of the water on Earth is salty and found in seas and oceans. The remainder is freshwater. Some of this is frozen into the great ice sheets of the Arctic and Antarctica, and mountain **glaciers**. The rest is found in lakes, rivers, streams, wetlands, in the soil as groundwater, and in the atmosphere as water vapor.

Shifting water We can think of all these places as storage houses for water, but water is constantly changing. It never remains the same because there are natural shifts between the water in the atmosphere and on the planet. This system, called the water cycle, keeps a balance between water in the air and on land.

Major rivers can even be seen from space. The Nile, the longest river in the world, is the thin strip to the left of this satellite image. It flows into the Mediterranean Sea, above.

Rivers Rivers have an important role in the water cycle because so much water finds its way into them, as rain or in other forms.

A river is a natural flow of water moving in a **channel** toward the sea. As it docs so, it constantly changes and shapes the landscape. This process happens over thousands of years.

Some rivers flow into lakes, marshes, or wetlands—but eventually all water ends up in the oceans.

Take it further

Investigate where rain collects after a shower. For example, you can make a puddle map of your school yard.

◆ Show if the puddles are large or small quantities of water.
◆ Try to find out why they collect where they do.

How the water cycle works

1 Most rain falls on the seas, oceans, rivers, and lakes. About a fifth falls on land. A certain amount of this will become groundwater by soaking into the soil and cracks in rocks. Some of the **groundwater** will find its way back into rivers. Water flows from rivers into the seas.

4 The clouds become thick with the droplets of moisture, until these droplets are so heavy that the water eventually falls as rain. If it is cold enough, the water falls as snow, sleet, or hail. In this way, the water cycle begins again.

2 Plants use up some groundwater and release some back into the air through a process called **transpiration**.

3 The sun warms surface water, both on land and in oceans, rivers, and lakes. As it is warmed, it **evaporates** and rises as water vapor, then cools and **condenses** to form clouds.

THE RIVER'S COURSE

Most rivers begin their journeys high in the mountains. Some start as trickles of water from melting glaciers, others from lakes or springs. A river may flow for thousands of miles across a continent. It may join a larger river, or other rivers may feed into it. It will pass through different landscapes, and perhaps through towns and cities. But a river will always move from high to low ground because its water is governed by **gravity**, and it will try to find the easiest route to the sea.

Mountain streams

When rain falls on a mountainside, it seeps into the soil and crevices in rocks. Once these are full, the water spills onto the surface, creating streams that travel down the mountainside. These are the **sources** of rivers.

A mountain stream flows into a river below.

Follow it through: a river's course

Source is on high ground; stream water is pulled down by gravity

Streams join to become a river, which also flows down mountains and hills

The upper course

A river's route has three stages. In its upper course it moves downstream, cutting a deep, narrow channel. The slope is often steep and rocky, and there are many obstacles in the river's path.

The middle course

Here the river has a deeper and wider channel. Other smaller rivers join the main one, increasing the amount of water the river carries. It will flow fastest when the river is full and has strong currents. Zigzag shapes, called **meanders**, develop across the flood plain—the area that can flood after heavy rain.

Take it further

Where is your nearest river?

◆ Find it on a map and trace its course.
◆ What part of the river is in your locality? The upper, middle, or lower course?
◆ What is the land surrounding the river used for?

The lower course

Toward the end of its course, the river has less energy and becomes slower. The part of the river that enters the sea— or sometimes a lake—is called the **mouth**.

A river's course

Source

Upper course

Middle course

Tributary river

Lower course

Watershed
(see *page 15*)

Flood plain

Meander

Oxbow lake
(see *page 20*)

Mouth

The river cuts a narrow channel downward and moves on to more even ground

The river forms meanders across the gentler sloping land

The river enters the sea or lake at its mouth

ERODING AND TRANSPORTING

A river may appear to be just a body of moving water, but there is a great deal of activity going on that affects its channel and surroundings.

Erosion As a river flows over rock and earth, it wears it away in a process called **erosion**. This takes place in several ways.

Corrasion occurs when material collides with the river's sides and bed. This also happens when pebbles grind into the bed causing potholes. They are carved into a circular shape by the river's action.

Corrosion occurs when rocks are dissolved by river water. This happens in particular to soft rocks such as chalk or limestone.

Another form of erosion is **attrition**. This happens when rocks, stones, and gravel crash into each other and break up into smaller pieces. Material worn away from the upper course of the river travels downstream, causing more erosion further down.

Finally, there is **hydraulic action**. This happens when the force of water is so great that it sweeps away materials from the sides and the bed of the river.

Follow it through: erosion → River flows quickly and picks up material → Material hits the river's banks → The banks and bed are eroded

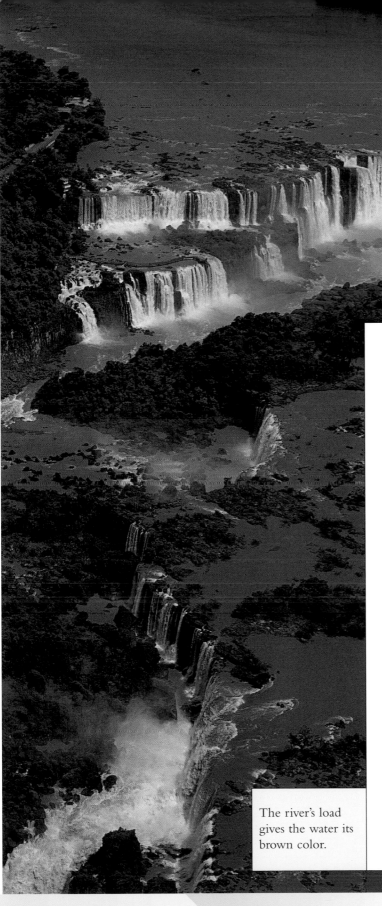

The river's load gives the water its brown color.

Take it further

Collect some river water and sediment in a jar. Shake or stir it and watch it settle.

◆ What materials can you see?
◆ Which settle first?
◆ Which do you think could be transported by suspension? (Always be careful if you are visiting a river site.)

Transportation

A river also moves its "load" of rocks, pebbles, earth, gravel, and other materials from one place to another: a process called **transportation**. This takes four different forms.

Some materials are dissolved in the water and carried in **solution**. Other small, visible particles are often light enough to be carried in **suspension** in a fast-flowing river.

Saltation occurs when small stones—too heavy to be lifted by the flow—jump along the riverbed. At the same time, larger rocks and stones are rolled or pushed along, becoming rounder and smoother, in a process called traction.

Fast and steep

The extent of erosion and transportation depends on several things: how much energy the river has, how much water it is carrying, and how steep the land is. Erosion and transportation also work together because the material the river transports helps the river to erode.

Eroded material breaks away from the banks and bed

This material is transported in the flow

Further erosion is caused by the river's load, as it flows along its course

DEPOSITING MATERIALS

In addition to eroding and transporting material, the river also deposits. This happens whenever the water lacks the energy to carry its load. There are certain points on the river's course where this occurs.

A river makes a looping meander.

Meanders These are bends or loops in the river created across the flood plain as the current swings from side to side. The water flows at different rates—quickly on the outside of a bend and more slowly on the inside. This causes the river to erode its banks on the outside, while dropping material on the inside, increasing the size of the bends. Over time, the meanders become larger and shift their position, changing the natural landscape.

Follow it through: deposition

River has less energy on some parts of its course

It drops its load

Spilling onto the flood plain A river carries its greatest load when it is full, usually after heavy rain.

If a river floods, its energy falls and it can no longer carry its load. Some is deposited on the river's banks, forming natural embankments called **levees**. Elsewhere, **silt**—fine soil—is dropped across the flood plain, helping to create fertile soil for farming.

Estuaries Material is also deposited at a river's mouth, where it enters the sea. Here, some rivers create **estuaries**—where deposits of silt and sand create mudflats or sandflats. If the river splits around the mudflats into channels, a **delta** is created (*see page 21*). Estuaries are flooded by the sea, but at low tide the mudflats are visible.

Deposits of silt have created mudflats at this river's estuary.

Lakes A river that has its mouth at a lake also drops its load. Its energy decreases as the water deepens. The heavier materials are dropped first, followed by the finer silt.

Over many years, these silt deposits can build up into layers, or jetties. On the Gippsland lake system in New South Wales, Australia, silt jetties formed around one million years ago. They stretch in long lines far into Lake King. Because of their shapes they are called finger deltas or bird's foot deltas.

The material forms slopes at the inner bend of a meander

Over time silt builds up on the inner bend

The river continues to erode the bank of the outer bend

The meander gets bigger

TRIBUTARIES AND DRAINAGE

A river is rarely just a single channel along its course. On its journey it is joined by other rivers, and may also split into separate channels itself. From source to mouth, rivers are ever-changing and dynamic.

Several tributaries flowing into this river create a shape like a tree, with branches across the landscape.

Coming together, splitting apart

Smaller rivers that join the main river are called **tributaries**. High in the mountains, these tributaries may be small streams called **headwaters**. Much larger tributaries—rivers in their own right—are found further along the river's course on the flood plain. The point where rivers meet is known as a **confluence**. Finally, at the mouth, the river discharges into the sea, and may separate into channels called distributaries.

The Nile's tributaries On the upstream section of the Nile, two major tributaries join to form the main river.

The White Nile begins at Lake Victoria in Uganda, and runs northward through lakes and swamps on a course of about 1,590 miles (2,560 km).

The Blue Nile flows 1,000 miles (1,600 km) from Lake Tana in Ethiopia, and meets the White Nile at Khartoum in the Sudan. The main part of the river Nile then runs for another 1,800 miles (3,000 km) to the Mediterranean Sea.

The drainage basin and watershed

The area of land drained by a river and its tributaries is called the **drainage basin**. This is the land that slopes down toward the river, with steep sides in the mountains, and gentler inclines as the river passes through its course. The Nile has a drainage area of 1,112,000 square miles (2,881,000 sq km).

The ridge of land in between two drainage basins is called the **watershed**. The area shown on the diagram on page 9 represents a drainage basin with an upland watershed.

Take it further
On a map choose a major river, such as the Amazon or the Yangtze.

◆ Find its tributaries. What are their names?
◆ Find a confluence.
◆ How many major cities does it flow through?

The Giant Amazon Some drainage basins are gigantic. The river Amazon is 4,000 miles (6,450 km) long, and although this is shorter than the Nile, it drains more than 2.7 million square miles (7 million sq km) of land. This is over 40 percent of the South American continent, and nearly two and a half times more area than the Nile.

The Amazon rises in the Andes Mountains and tumbles down in great waterfalls and rapids, dropping thousands of feet. Many tributaries join it over its course from west to east, arriving at the Atlantic Ocean. At its mouth, the Amazon is over 148 miles (240 km) wide.

The Orinoco River is a tributary of the Amazon. Its basin extends over 58,000 square miles (150,000 sq km). It is divided between Brazil and Venezuela.

RIVER VALLEYS

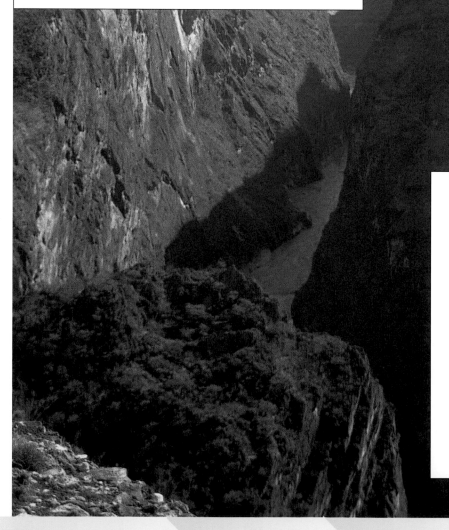

Some of the most dramatic landforms are river valleys. These are shaped over thousands of years, and have different characteristics according to where the valley occurs on the river's route. There are many kinds of river valleys, but they all follow the same basic pattern of development.

Tiger-leaping Gorge, a "V"-shaped valley in China.

Highland valleys

On its upper course, a river will cut deep into the land, eroding downward so there is little or no valley floor. This, along with the weather's action, erodes the valley's sides to make a "V" shape, giving rise to the name "V"-shaped valley. Many of the steepest and longest river valleys are in the Himalayas of Asia. Some have sides that plunge nearly 5,000 feet (1,500 m).

Follow it through: valley erosion

River runs through a valley ➤ Water erodes the valley sides ➤ Drainage basin increases

Spurs As the river erodes downward, it begins to twist and turn around hard rock, forming sections of land, called "spurs," jutting into the valley. The spurs alternate from side to side, and from a great height, they often look as if they should fit neatly into each other, like pieces in a jigsaw puzzle. This gives them the name "interlocking spurs."

Lesser gradients
Further changes occur as the river makes its way downhill. When tributaries flow into the river and its channel becomes wider, it erodes sideways into the river banks in addition to eroding downward. This creates a valley floor and flat land. Now there are slopes instead of steep gradients, and a wider "V"-shaped valley.

Moffat Valley in Scotland. The river meanders along the valley floor.

Lowland valleys As the river flows nearer to the sea, its meandering course pushes out the valley sides still further. Some rivers, such as the Mississippi and the Hwang Ho in China, have huge meanders that sweep across the valley. These are created by the rivers' action, which is both eroding and depositing material (*see pages 12–13*). These processes continually widen the valley floor.

Over time, the river creates its **flood plain**. On the river's lower course, the valley sides can hardly be seen, if at all.

More water runs off into the river

River has more power

Valley is eroded further, including the river's floor

WATERFALLS AND RAPIDS

One of the most spectacular of all river features—and perhaps in all nature—is a waterfall. Some are special because of their beauty, particularly when they drop from a great height. Others stand out because of the great rush and power of the flowing water. A few of the greatest waterfalls are impressive for both reasons.

The creation of a waterfall
Waterfalls are created by erosion. The river meets hard rock, then flows onto soft rock. The water erodes soft rock far more quickly, so the hard rock is left extending out as a ledge that the water spills over.

A small upstream waterfall in the Swiss Alps.

Foz do Iguaçu Park Falls, Brazil.

Moving waterfalls
Waterfalls spill into a plunge pool, which is eroded by the water and the material it transports as it pours down. In addition, boulders and stones from the edge fall into the pool and the ledge breaks away. Consequently, over thousands of years, the waterfall slowly shifts backwards.

Waterfalls can be tiny or immense. The Iguaçu River in Brazil forms a vast network of 275 separate waterfalls in the Foz do Iguaçu National Park. Plunging nearly 270 feet (82 m), they are some of the world's most impressive and beautiful waterfalls.

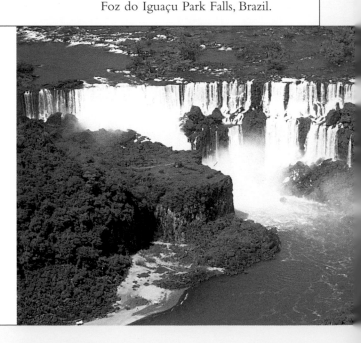

Follow it through: waterfalls

River meets hard rock and soft rock

Soft rock is eroded first

Case study: Niagara Falls, U.S. and Canada

River landscape features can be so dramatic and important that they become borders between one country and another. The Niagara Falls form a boundary between Canada and the U.S. It consists of two main waterfalls separated by Goat Island.

Influence on the area

Although only the 49th highest waterfall in the world, the Niagara Falls is the third greatest in terms of the power and volume of water. Its spectacular beauty makes it one of North America's major tourist attractions. This has caused the entire area to be developed for tourism, including parks, golf-courses, museums, shops, and restaurants. Without the draw of the waterfall, the area would be very different.

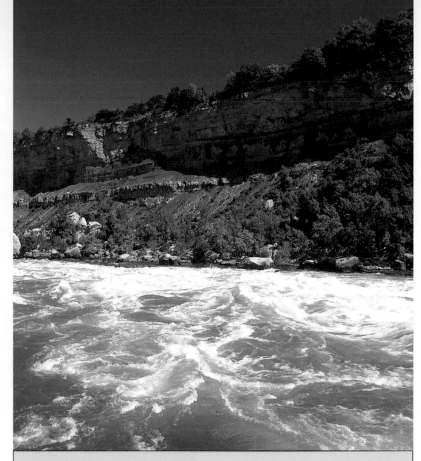

Great Gorge Adventure Rapids, Niagara, Canada.

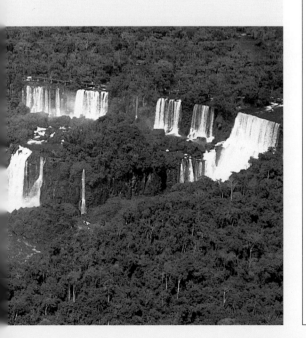

Rapids Rapids are created in a way similar to waterfalls. Where water rushes over bands of soft and hard rock on the river bed, the soft rock is worn away first. This leaves the hard rock to form a series of steps, like small waterfalls, on the river bed. Where there are steep steps, the eddies and currents can be fierce. The steps may become so steep that the rapids eventually develop into a waterfall. A region of rapids usually remains in the stretch immediately upstream from a waterfall, such as Niagara Falls.

Rapids like these are used for recreational or sporting activities such as white water rafting. The river Ocoee in Tennessee was once harnessed for water power. An artificial channel called a "flume" diverted the water to a power plant, but this made the river unusable for people. The flume was eventually disbanded and the rapids restored.

A ledge of hard rock is left jutting out ➤ A waterfall is created ➤ The ledge breaks away ➤ Waterfall moves backwards

OXBOWS AND DELTAS

Other spectacular landscape features are formed by the river's action further along its course.

Crescent-shaped lakes

As the river zigzags across its flood plain, eroding land on the outer bend of the meander and depositing material on the inner (*see pages 12-13*), the loops it makes become circular and very large, with a narrow neck.

At a certain point the river cuts through the land at the neck of the loop, taking a straight, more direct course. A crescent-shaped lake called an **oxbow** is left behind (*see diagram on page 9*).

An aerial view of a tightly meandering river in Borneo. The river will eventually cut through at the "neck," leaving behind the meander as an oxbow lake.

Follow it through: oxbow lakes

River erodes on its outer bend

It deposits on its inner bend

Meanders form

Mud and sand

Mud and sand Further deposits of mud and sand, called deltas, can form around estuaries. Triangular-shaped deltas occur over vast areas at the mouths of large rivers, where the currents are slow and there are no strong tides to wash the silt away. Because the deposits block up the mouth, the river splits into two channels that flow around the blockage.

Further channels occur in this way as the water attempts to reach the sea.

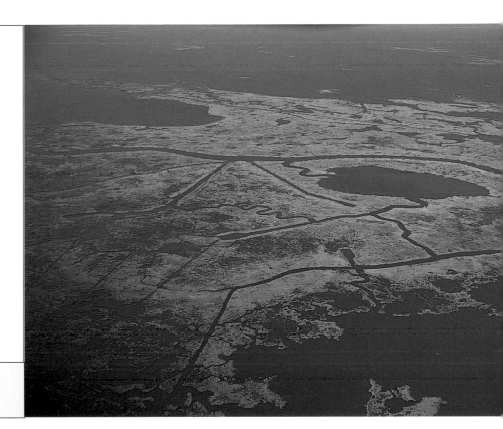

The Mississippi delta between Houma and Grand Isle, Louisiana.

Stagnant rivers The river Ganges, in India, is estimated to carry 900,000 tons of sediment daily. Not surprisingly, its huge low-lying delta is continually growing, and the landscape changes as channels silt up. Parts of the delta are made up of older deposits that have been cut into by the current distributary rivers.

At some point, probably a few centuries ago, the main outlet of the river moved from west to east, leaving the western part as a "dying" delta of stagnant rivers and poor soils that are not renewed by fertile silt.

A satellite view of the mouth of the river Ganges in Bangladesh. Silt deposits have been cut into separate banks by the many distributary rivers.

| In time, meanders become bigger | The sides of the loop get closer | The neck of the loop is cut through | An oxbow lake is left behind |

RIVER SETTLEMENTS

Many major settlements had their beginnings by rivers. Although a site was chosen for its easy access to food or for its defensive position, rivers may continue to be just as important to towns and cities today.

Egypt's growth The Nile, the world's longest river, has seen settlements grow around it for thousands of years. Floods created fertile land for farming, and a regular supply of food meant that communities grew.

The northern part of the Nile flows through Egypt, one of the longest continuously settled places on Earth. There, in the river valley, the ancient Egyptian civilization began around 7,000 years ago. Today, Egypt is still centered on the Nile. Some 99 percent of Egypt's population lives in the Nile's basin, and depends on agriculture that requires irrigation from the river.

Case study: New Orleans

The city of New Orleans owes much of its success to the Mississippi River, the longest river in the U.S.

Busy port

After its discovery in 1541, the Mississippi became a major transportation route for goods such as crops and furs, and the busy port of New Orleans grew up around it.

Tourism

Today the city is still a busy port, but the river now also provides recreational facilities such as boating, fishing, and swimming. This attracts tourists to the city, so the Mississippi continues to be New Orleans' lifeline.

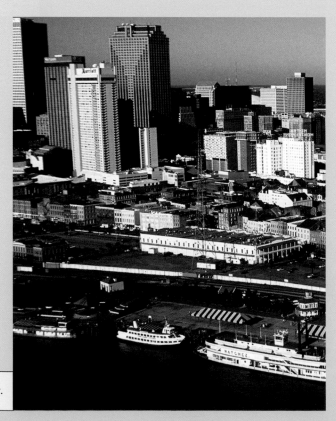

New Orleans on the Mississippi River.

Follow it through: new settlers → Land taken by settlers → Not always enough water for the growing population → Large irrigation projects introduced

Running dry   Rivers are often the main reason why an area is settled in hot, dry regions; but sometimes rivers also dry up during droughts. In order to survive, people have learned how to adapt the environment.

The river Murray, which runs through parts of the southwestern Australian outback, has a history of drying up. The area was first settled by Aborigines, who were thought to have lived along parts of the river for at least 25,000 years. During periods when the river dried up, the Aborigines conserved water in rock holes.

River irrigation has enabled vineyards to prosper in Australia.

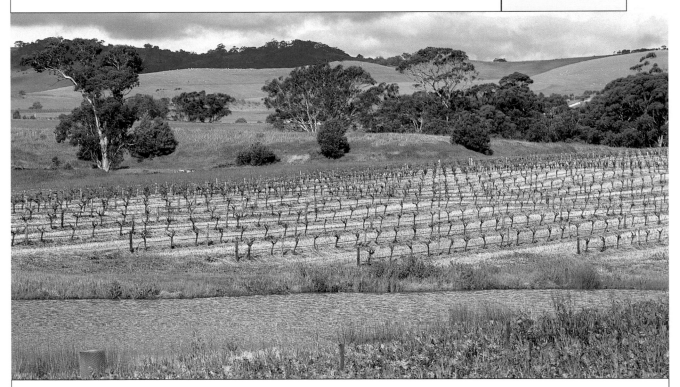

Surviving the climate   With the coming of European settlers, the Aborigines lost their lands. The river Murray now became the main transportation route bringing goods to the new settlements. But the settlers faced the same problems as the Aborigines—surviving in the harsh climate.

Only when large-scale irrigation projects were introduced did any of these settlements survive. Taking the water from the river and pumping or channeling it onto the land created fertile soil. The region now provides most of southwestern Australia with huge quantities of produce from orchards and vineyards. The river has allowed settlements to grow and prosper despite the harsh climate.

Land becomes fertile ▶ Orchards and vineyards flourish ▶ Area changes and becomes an agricultural region

IRRIGATING FARMLAND

Rivers are essential to farmers. Over thousands of years, farmers have developed many ways to use rivers for irrigation, but the most modern methods have probably had the greatest impact on rivers and the landscape.

Different irrigation methods

In the simplest forms of irrigation, water is drawn from a river and distributed over the land by means of small ditches. This method is used by individual farmers in arid countries all over the world.

Larger communities have more complicated systems in which rivers supply canals, and the canals form branches that carry the water to all parts of the cultivated region. The largest irrigation systems involve the development of entire river basins with canals, dams, and other major engineering works. They have a massive impact on the landscape.

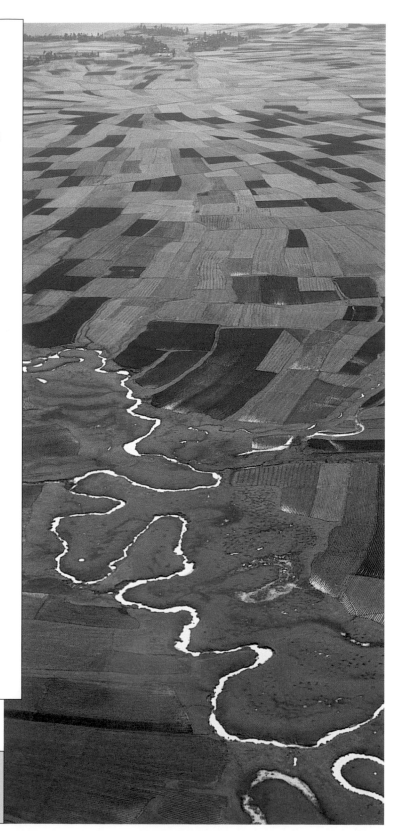

An aerial view of a river meandering through irrigated land in Ethiopia. A single river can be used to irrigate a vast area of land.

Follow it through: irrigation

Where there is little rainfall, farmers take river water

This is passed through channels to irrigate the soil

Supplying a large area

Modern irrigation systems, supplied by rivers, are capable of feeding millions of acres of land. Most of the irrigation water in India and Pakistan is supplied by tributaries of the Indus and Ganges rivers, and is distributed by one of the best-developed canal systems in the world. This system irrigates a vast area of land.

Irrigation problems
Modern irrigation systems control the flow of a river, so there is always just enough water. While this prevents flooding, it can also cause problems.

The Nile is Egypt's main source of irrigation. In the past, annual floods irrigated the area and carried silt—fine fertile soil—onto the land. Modern systems now provide year-round irrigation, but stop the annual flooding. This reduces the silt renewal, requiring farmers to buy expensive fertilizer to enrich the soil.

Irrigation channels can have mixed results. This Egyptian field (*above*) has become waterlogged due to over-irrigation, and without the annual flooding, there are fewer areas of fertile land such as this flood plain in Luxor (*below*).

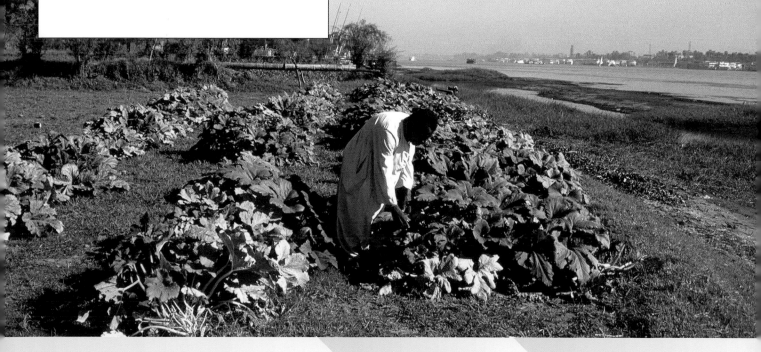

Crops can be watered all year round

No silt from regular flooding

Soil is less rich and there are fewer fish

Fertilizers are needed

DAMS

The first simple dams were clay or stone banks across rivers. Their purpose was to hold back the flow of water so that a small lake formed. This could be used to irrigate fields or trap fish. Such dams had a limited effect on the surrounding landscape. Modern dams have many more functions and work on a much greater scale. As a result, they have more wide-ranging effects.

Modern dams These are huge, expensive projects that take many years to build. They are usually built in an upland area where there is a steep-sided valley, gorge, or canyon; some hard rock; and a regular flow of water. The dam holds back the river so that the water level behind it rises. The surrounding landscape is flooded and a deep **reservoir** or lake is created. The flow of water is usually controlled by **sluice gates** and the water can be used to irrigate land, prevent floods, and generate power (*see water power, page 30*).

The problem with dams Dams have many benefits, but they also create problems. The main one is that they change the landscape beyond recognition. Towns and villages can be wiped out by the creation of a lake, and wildlife habitats destroyed.

Because the dam blocks the river, it prevents the navigation of shipping and migration by fish, although special channels can be built to help. The creation of an artificial lake can also bring benefits, such as a providing a site for recreation and encouraging wildlife.

A dam in Australia has caused this river to flood rainforest and bush land.

Follow it through: dams

Dams block rivers → They hold back the flow of water → A lake is created behind the dam

Take it further

Find out the effect the Three Gorges Dam has on the town of Yichang. Start by searching the website: www.riverdeep.net.

◆ What happens to the people and local businesses?
◆ What could the Chinese government do about this?

Case study: the Three Gorges Dam, China

The Three Gorges Dam is a massive, controversial project begun in 1992 and due to be completed in 2009. It is being built at Sandouping on the river Yangtze, one of the longest rivers in the world. The project is intended to create electricity and prevent flooding. It will also allow ships to pass through the three gorges—Wu, Xiling, and Qutang—more easily.

Landscape changes

There will be a huge impact on the surrounding area, particularly when the land is flooded to create a lake. Villages and towns will be drowned in the rising waters, and two million people will need new homes. Factories and industries will disappear, and wildlife will be destroyed. The area is also an earthquake zone, and there are fears that a serious earthquake might undermine the dam. Millions of gallons of water could be released with disastrous results.

The Three Gorges Dam is a massive engineering project.

| The flow of water from the lake into the river is controlled | Water is used for power and irrigation | Landscape is changed |

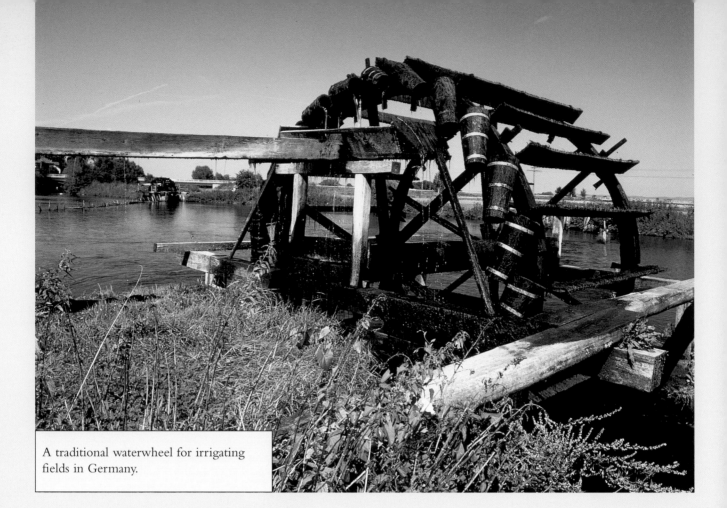

A traditional waterwheel for irrigating fields in Germany.

WATER POWER

River water has been used to generate power for thousands of years. The waterwheel was first used by the Romans, and became a familiar feature of many landscapes until the 20th century. Today, dams are used to create hydroelectric power, dramatically affecting the rivers and the surrounding landscape.

Waterwheels Waterwheels were mainly used in the past to run mills that ground grain into flour. For small scale use, they were clean and reliable. The small millpond (created as the river was dammed) not only provided the water to drive the wheel, but also attracted birds, frogs, dragonflies, and other creatures.

Compared to modern systems of water power, the waterwheel had little impact on the river and the surrounding environment.

Hydroelectric power Modern methods use water to create hydroelectric power—energy produced by falling water. In mountain regions where the water is fast-flowing, its energy can be used directly to drive turbines and create electricity.

Once a dam has been built, the water in the reservoir behind the dam is usually controlled by sluice gates. When these are opened water rushes out, passes down pipes, and drives a turbine that produces electricity in a generator. The electricity is sent along pylons to homes, factories, and offices.

Case study: Waikato River, New Zealand

The Waikato is New Zealand's longest river, on which eight dams with power plants have been built. This has led to great changes in the surrounding landscape.

Using the lakes

The plants provide much of the power for New Zealand's North Island. The artificial lakes have also been given an extra purpose by becoming popular recreational areas that attract thousands of visitors each year. Before the development of the dams, the fast-moving river allowed for only a limited range of activities.

Take it further

Carry out some research into two different dams—a small one and a large one.

◆ How much power does each generate?
◆ What effect on the local environment does each one have?
◆ Which do you think is more successful?

Water passing through the Victoria Dam in Sri Lanka creates a massive force that is harnessed for hydroelectric power.

Alternative energy

Hydroelectric power has certain advantages over other ways of producing energy. It does not rely on fossil fuels, such as coal, which create pollution. It is also a renewable source. This means it can be replaced and is not constantly being used up.

Its main disadvantage is its reliance on dams, which disrupt the local landscape and are costly to build.

RIVERS AS WATERWAYS

Rivers have been used for transportation for thousands of years. They provided a natural network across land when roads were only tracks. However, traveling by river was limited because rapid and shallow waters were often impossible to navigate. As a result, people found ways to alter rivers to overcome these problems.

The Mississippi River, the longest river in the U.S., has long been an important transportation route. In parts it is over a mile wide, and its depth ranges between 50-100 feet (15–30 m).

Straighter and deeper Rivers such as the Mississippi have been straightened to cut out meanders. Channels have been deepened by removing the silt deposits—a process called dredging. These measures increase the river's flow, which allows vessels to travel more quickly and directly.

But these kinds of changes come at a price. Deepening and shortening the river's channel can increase the volume and speed of the water downstream. This means that the chances of flooding in heavy rain become greater. In the case of the Mississippi, erosion increased as the flow became quicker, and the river dumped more silt downstream. This caused the river to meander once again.

Canals These are constructed waterways that can bypass obstacles to connect one river with another, or a river with a sea. They are massive engineered constructions and may even include aqueducts—bridges that carry water—to take vessels over valleys and ravines.

Take it further
Using a map of the country, plan a route for a new canal that connects two river systems.

◆ What problems will you have to overcome?
◆ What landscape features will be lost?
◆ What benefits might it bring?

A narrowboat passes over Pontcysyllte Aqueduct on the Shropshire Union Canal in Clwyd, Wales, UK. This canal, like many others, is now used largely by leisure boats.

Major canals Canals have given us a network of water transportation to carry cargo across continents. The Panama Canal connects the Atlantic and the Pacific oceans; the Europa Canal connects the rivers Rhine and Danube. The Rhine is also linked to the Saone, the main tributary of the Rhone, by canals. These waterways are very important for shipping, and are constantly being used by barges carrying raw materials.

Building canals The building of canals causes widespread destruction of landscapes and habitats. Disused canals can also cause problems because they attract waste and pollution. These canals can be renewed, however, and may become popular leisure areas.

WHEN RIVERS FLOOD

Flooding rivers are a major concern. They occur for many reasons, but can often be caused by a landscape change, such as deforestation, the building of hard surfaces, or the restructuring of a river's course.

The river Jhelum in Srinagar, Kashmir, has a history of flooding. Many people have now made their homes on houseboats.

When floods happen

River floods may occur in any season, but they are more likely in spring and in winter. In the spring, the main causes of flooding are heavy rains and a rise in temperature. In the winter, the main factors are frozen soil, deep snow, and a thaw. Floods during winter and spring occur on major rivers and affect large areas.

Follow it through: deforestation

Trees are cut down

Soil is no longer held by tree roots

Rainy days Rivers often overflow in heavy rain. This can happen when the ground is already waterlogged. The excess water runs into rivers, which rise and burst their banks. The area of land that is most likely to flood is across the flood plain, since this is the lowest lying area on a river's course. This is also the area where many people live. Settlements originated on flood plains because the soil was fertile and the land flat.

The increased building of roads, sidewalks, parking lots, and other hard surfaces means that excess water is not absorbed by the soil. Instead, it runs into drains and into the rivers, eventually causing a flood. Heavy rain combined with a high tide can be especially destructive.

Deforestation
The destruction of forests can also have an effect on rivers. When trees are cleared, their roots no longer hold the soil and this can cause erosion. Heavy rain then washes away the topsoil into the rivers. The soil builds up, the rivers become blocked, and flooding occurs. This is a particular problem in countries that are being cleared of rainforest.

Changing a river's course
Dramatic changes to a river by people can also have unforeseen effects. The Netherlands suffered from catastrophic floods in 1993 and 1995. These can be traced to the straightening of the upper Rhine to improve shipping conditions. This led to rising waters flowing downstream more rapidly (*see page 40*).

Floods can cause millions of dollars worth of damage to homes and other property.

Benefits and disasters
Floods can also be beneficial. Bangladesh experiences both the benefits and the disasters of flooding from rivers and the sea. The country is situated on the flat, broad Ganges delta. Like the land along the Nile, fertile soil is produced by the silt carried in the floodwaters, so it is good for farming. Farmers are able to produce enough food for the region's large population.

However, the rainy season—known as the monsoon—can bring disaster. The rivers burst their banks and submerge farmland in a great sweep of water. Thousands can die along with their livestock, and crops can be destroyed.

In response, people have turned to ways to defend against flooding.

Heavy rain washes topsoil into rivers > Soil builds up in the river > Rivers become blocked and flood during heavy rain

FLOOD CONTROL

Flooding can never be completely prevented but it can be controlled, especially with modern flood forecasting methods. These involve studying how a river is likely to react during particular kinds of weather. Satellites send pictures showing conditions in the atmosphere. Data is collected, fed into a computer, and a forecast is made. Flood protection is then used at the right time.

The Thames Flood Barrier was opened in 1982 to prevent flooding in central London during high tides and winds.

Dams and barriers

Large scale **hard engineering** projects such as dams and barriers, which hold back a river and manage its flow, can be highly effective at flood control. The Thames Flood Barrier in London is a striking landmark across the river. It has steel gates that can be opened or closed, and can endure pressure of up to 9,000 tons.

Concrete levees

Other hard-engineering methods, such as **dikes** or concrete embankments (levees), are built alongside rivers to keep the river in its course. About 30,000 square miles (78,000 sq km) of the flood plain of the Mississippi River are protected by levees and other structures. They have to be constantly renewed or increased in height.

Follow it through: soft-engineering flood control

Marshlands renewed

They take in and hold rainwater

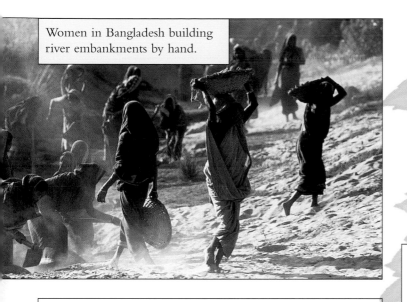

Women in Bangladesh building river embankments by hand.

Take it further

Many of those living on the world's great deltas, such as those in Bangladesh and China, depend on farming. Find out what methods are being proposed to help reduce flooding.

◆ Are they nature-friendly or not?
◆ What effect might they have on the landscape?

Dredging Because of the enormous load of silt that the Hwang Ho (or Yellow River) carries, it is very wide and shallow. This has led to so many disastrous floods that the river is often called "China's Sorrow."

To prevent further floods, the river's bed has been dredged to lower it, and embankments have been built. In some stretches during high rainfall, the water level between the embankments may be 30 feet (9 m) above the surrounding plain.

These changes have a huge impact on the environment. For that reason, alternative **soft-engineering** methods, such as terracing and reforestation, are becoming more popular.

Dredging the Yellow River to remove silt.

Controlling run-off Terracing is a form of irrigation usually found in upland areas. It involves cutting a series of steps into the hillside, so that the farmed land is almost level, rather than on a slope. In addition to being a good farming method, it can be used as flood control: rainwater is collected so **run-off** into rivers is limited.

Other methods to control water run-off and prevent flooding include planting trees on hillsides and digging small irrigation channels on farmland.

Protecting wetlands In the past, draining wetlands—low-lying marshy regions—led to flooding, since the marshland acts as a reservoir for heavy rains. **Conservation** projects to renew wetlands help to prevent flooding, and also revive the natural vegetation and support wildlife.

Like dams and barriers, these soft-engineering projects can alter landscapes. However, they do so in a way that encourages sensible farming and balances the needs of the people, plants, and animals in the environment.

Less water run-off into rivers

Reduces flooding

Environment for wildlife restored

POLLUTED RIVERS

Rivers have always been used to dump waste, but as the world's population has grown, pollution has increased. Despite greater awareness, pollution still reaches rivers and groundwater in several ways, damaging the landscape and the environment.

Chemicals discharged into a river affect the water and can harm plant and animal life.

Sources of pollution The main sources of river pollution are farm waste—especially fertilizers—industrial waste, oil, and even warm water. Waste can also produce poisons that seep into groundwater. All these things change the water, usually decreasing the oxygen available to support plant and animal life.

Follow it through: cost of river pollution

Farmers and industries want to dispose of waste cheaply

Cleaning up rivers

Several things can be done to improve river quality. Fines for industrial pollution can be strictly enforced. Natural farming methods that do not use artificial fertilizers, such as organic farming, can be encouraged. Greater **recycling** of garbage is also important.

If a polluted river is cleaned, nature quickly returns. British rivers were once some of the worst in Europe. Many are now cleaner than they have been for 150 years. This is partly due to the decline in heavy industry, but also due to stricter pollution controls and programs to clean up rivers.

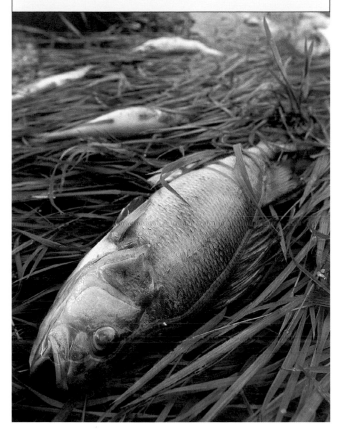

Industrial waste pumped into rivers can harm wildlife.

Volunteers clear dumped waste from a river's edge.

Case study: the Illinois River

The surrounding flood plains of the Illinois River are used mainly for raising crops. Formerly, the river was highly productive: it produced 10 percent of the U.S. freshwater fish catch. By the 1970s, the same stretch of river produced only 0.32 percent of the total freshwater fish harvest.

This was due to two major factors: the diversion of Chicago's sewage from Lake Michigan to the river, and the high level of agriculture—the fertilizers caused a reduction in the oxygen levels. This pollution is slowly being reversed with new sewage treatment methods.

| Fertilizers and chemicals are dumped into rivers | Supply of freshwater decreases and wildlife is harmed | Costly river clean-up is needed |

The junction of the river Rhine and the Mosel in Germany.

Rivers are damaged not only by pollution. Changing the course of the river, building dams, embankments, and large irrigation projects often have unexpected outcomes for the river and the surrounding landscape. Many governments now accept that controlling rivers for human use should be balanced against the damage this can cause to the environment.

Rhine 2020 Attempts to improve the Rhine caused disastrous flooding (*see page 35*). Now, a project called Rhine 2020 has been undertaken to protect and renew the river. Its name refers to the time span of the project—20 years from its start in 2000.

The goals of the project are to lower the water levels on the straightened stretch of the Rhine, and restore wetlands, which are a natural water purifier and help reduce flooding (*see pages 42–43*). Already, improvements have been made to the water quality of the river. Wildlife along the riverbanks is starting to return.

But the Rhine is still a major waterway, and ensuring the river revives while maintaining it as a transportation route requires careful planning.

Follow it through: changes to a river bank

Trees are cut on a river bank ▸ Giant reeds grow ▸ Reeds block up the river and cannot provide shade

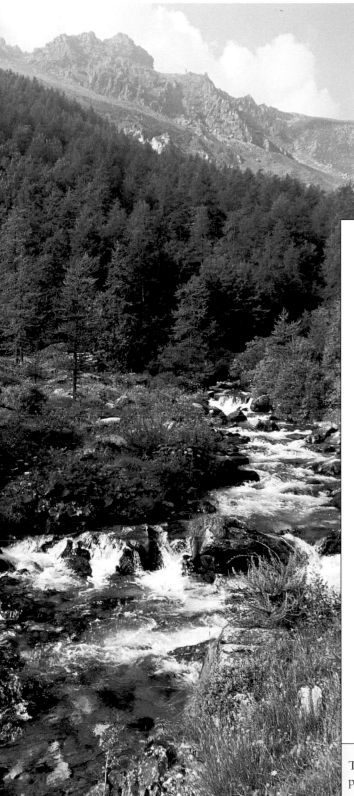

Take it further

Find out how your nearest river is managed.

◆ Is it polluted or clean?
◆ Who is responsible for managing the river?
◆ What are their plans for the future?
◆ How will this affect the river and surrounding landscape?

Surrounding landscape   Another way to protect a river is to ensure that its surroundings are preserved or renewed.

The Santa Clara River in Southern California is protected by an environmental management plan. The plan involves limiting future building—particularly across the flood plain—and planting trees to replace the overhanging willows and cottonwood forests that have been cut down. The loss of these trees reduced the shade on the river, making the water temperature rise and the chemical balance of the river change. This allowed **algae** to flourish on the surface of the water. Algae starved fish and other wildlife of oxygen, and many died. The replanting plan has reversed this effect, and the river is now healthy and teeming with life.

Changing population   Other rivers are renewed less by design than by a simple change of circumstance. The upper Po Valley in Italy lost two-thirds of its population in the 1960s due to migration to cities. With fewer people, the river Po's waters have been renewed and wildlife has returned.

The clear, fresh waters of the river Po, Italy. The changing population has helped to renew all sections of the river.

Water temperature rises ▶ Algae flourishes ▶ Fish and other wildlife are starved of oxygen ▶ River renewal is needed

PROTECTING WETLANDS

The regeneration of wetlands is one way to prevent flooding, but they are in themselves very important **habitats**. Wetlands are low-lying marshy regions, fed by freshwater from rivers or streams and from tides near the coast. They support a wide variety of plant and animal life.

Wetlands and fish

From prehistoric times, people have used marshes for food for themselves and their animals.

It is estimated that 80 to 90 percent of the fish eaten throughout the world today depend on shallow coastal waters. Shrimp, crabs, oysters, and clams all depend on tidal and freshwater marshes for food and shelter, and in turn the fish attract many bird species.

The Burdekin wetland complex in North Queensland, Australia.

Case study 1: The Great Fen, East Anglia, UK

A great stretch of land across the eastern side of England was once covered by marshland called the Fens. It was first drained by the Romans and much of it has been used for farming ever since.

Big project

The Great Fen Project is attempting to restore some of this marshland, making it the largest conservation project in the UK in over 100 years. It will connect two important habitats, Woodwalton Fen and Holme Fen, making one large site. Farmland has been bought, and drains and ditches that kept the land dry for crops will be blocked to increase the water level. Extra water can be pumped from nearby rivers. It is hoped that natural fen grasses will reappear, followed by fen reeds, and later plants such as fen violets. As the habitat is slowly recreated, the area should become a haven for many birds and animals.

Follow it through: renewing wetlands → Farmland is purchased → Drains and ditches are blocked

Case study 2: The Everglades, Florida

The Everglades is an unusual area of wetland. It is a shallow but wide area that creeps slowly through southern Florida to the Gulf of Mexico. It has been called the "river of grass" and there is nowhere else on Earth quite like it. Great sweeps of grasses and mangrove forests hide endangered species such as alligators.

Wetland loss

For many years the Everglades was drained and developed, and the Kissimmee River, which fed it, was straightened and canaled. Nearly 50 percent of the Everglades was lost.

Restoration

Now it is a vast nature reserve, which is internationally valued. Projects to maintain and restore further areas of the Everglades are also being proposed.

Working with rivers

There is now a greater awareness of the need to restore rivers and waterways. This renews the landscape, sometimes returning it to the way it was thousands of years ago. Sustaining rivers also means that they can still be used as valuable resources. But to do this it must be recognized that rivers are dynamic. They are constantly changing and not easily tamed. The key is to work with them, not against them.

The Everglades is a wilderness that is unique in the U.S. Its diverse habitats support a huge array of wildlife. Some plants and animals do not exist anywhere else in the country.

The water level rises, creating marshland

Extra water can be pumped from rivers

Wildlife habitats return

GLOSSARY

Algae   Simple green plants that grow on ponds and rivers.

Attrition   Erosion caused by rocks crashing into each other.

Channel   The passage between two banks along which a river flows.

Condensation   Droplets of water from the air that form when the temperature falls.

Confluence   The place where two rivers meet.

Conservation   Protecting the environment.

Corrasion   Erosion caused by rocks colliding with a river bed and banks.

Corrosion   Erosion caused by chemicals in river water dissolving rock.

Defensive site   A site that offers protection from attack.

Delta   Low, flat land formed by silt deposits at a river's mouth.

Deposition   Material that is dropped by a river.

Drainage basin   The area drained by a river and its tributaries.

Dikes   Embankments built to keep a river in its channel to control flooding.

Erosion   The process of being slowly worn away.

Estuary   The mouth of a river that widens as the river flows into the sea.

Evaporation   The process of water changing from liquid to vapor.

Flood plain   The flat plain on each side of a river that often floods.

Glacier   A slow-moving river of ice.

Gravity   The force that pulls everything toward Earth.

Groundwater   Underground water stored in rock.

Habitat   A natural environment for plants and animals.

Hard engineering   Large-scale structural developments that change the environment.

Headwaters   Small streams that come together to form the start of a river.

Hydraulic action   Erosion caused by the force of water sweeping through a river.

Levees   Embankments along a river.

Meander   A bend or loop in a river.

Mouth   The place where a river flows into the ocean, sea, lake, or swamp.

Oxbow lake   A crescent-shaped lake formed when the loop of a river is cut off from the rest of the river.

Recycle   To process and reuse waste.

Reservoir   A lake built to store water, sometimes behind a dam.

Run-off	Rainwater carried away from an area by streams and rivers.
Saltation	Materials jumping along a river bed.
Silt	Fine, fertile soil that can be carried by a river.
Sluice gate	A gate for controlling the flow of water.
Soft engineering	Structural changes that work with the environment rather than against it.
Solution	Dissolved materials in the water of a river.
Source	The place where a river begins.
Suspension	Materials being carried by the flow of a river.
Transpiration	The process of water vapor passing into the air from plants and trees.
Transportation	The movement of materials by a river.
Tributary	A smaller river that flows into a larger river.
Watershed	The border between two drainage basins.

FURTHER INFORMATION

U.S. Environmental Protection Agency
Information on programs to protect and restore American rivers and streams.

www.epa.gov/owen/rivers.html

Rivernet
An organization that supports local communities in their efforts to protect and restore rivers, lakes, wetlands, and estuaries.

www.rivernetwork.org

International Rivers Network
A campaigning group that works to protect the world's rivers. Suitable for older students.

www.irn.org

National Geographic Society
A website that includes an interactive river system and river conservation activities.

www.nationalgeographic.com/geographyaction/rivers

World Wide Fund for Nature (WWF)
An organization concerned with conservation. Suitable for older students.

www.panda.org

More information on rivers
This website features many topics, including user-friendly information about rivers.

www.socialstudiesforkids.com

INDEX